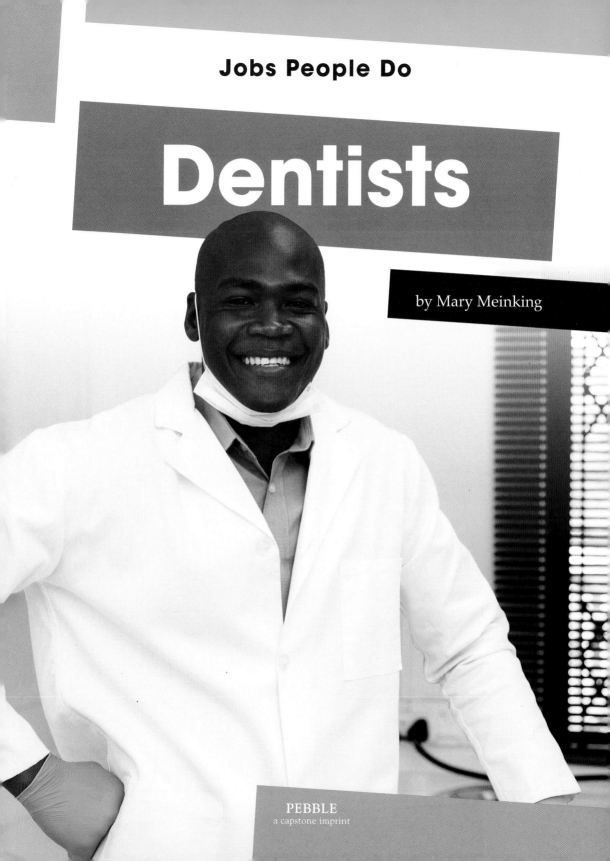

Jobs People Do

Dentists

by Mary Meinking

PEBBLE
a capstone imprint

Pebble Explore is published by Pebble, an imprint of Capstone.
1710 Roe Crest Drive
North Mankato, Minnesota 56003
www.capstonepub.com

Library of Congress Cataloging-in-Publication Data is available on the Library of Congress website.
ISBN: 978-1-9771-2346-6 (hardcover)
ISBN: 978-1-9771-2662-7 (paperback)
ISBN: 978-1-9771-2352-7 (eBook PDF)

Summary: Open wide! Dentists care for people's teeth. Give readers the inside scoop on what it's like to be a dentist. Readers will learn what dentists do, the tools they use, and how people get this exciting job.

Image Credits
Alamy: The History Collection, 28; Shutterstock: Andrey_Popov, 19, Dragon Images, Cover, Erica Smit, 9, karelnoppe, 23, luckyraccoon, 21, michaeljung, 1, Mikhail Kadochnikov, 12, Monkey Business Images, 22, Photographee.eu, 25, 27, RossHelen, 11, SofikoS, 7, Solis Images, 5, wavebreakmedia, 17, 18, worawit_j, 8, Yuri Bathan (yuri10b), 13; U.S. Air Force Photo: Airman 1st Class Megan Munoz, 14–15

Editorial Credits
Editor: Gena Chester; Designer: Kyle Grenz; Media Researcher: Jo Miller; Production Specialist: Spencer Rosio

All internet sites appearing in back matter were available and accurate when this book was sent to press.

Printed in the United States
PO117

Table of Contents

Words in **bold** are in the glossary.

What Is a Dentist?

Do you want **healthy** teeth? You need to brush and **floss**. You also need to visit a dentist. A dentist is a doctor for teeth. Dentists make sure teeth and **gums** stay healthy. Sometimes a tooth gets sore. Dentists know how to fix it. They make the tooth strong again. With a dentist's help, anyone can have a healthy smile!

What Dentists Do

Dentists are good at solving problems. They check teeth and gums. They see if anything is wrong. A dentist decides the best way to treat someone. They look at ways to fix teeth.

Dentists count children's teeth. They check new teeth that are growing.

Dentists teach people how to care
for their teeth. They show people how
to brush and floss. They teach people
about foods that are good and bad for
teeth too.

Some teeth have soft spots. These are **cavities**!

Cavities need to be filled. A dentist removes the soft spot on the tooth. Then they place a hard **filling** in the tooth. This makes the tooth strong again.

Dentists put a clear **sealant** on teeth. It keeps cavities from starting.

Sometimes a tooth gets knocked out. A dentist can put in a fake tooth.

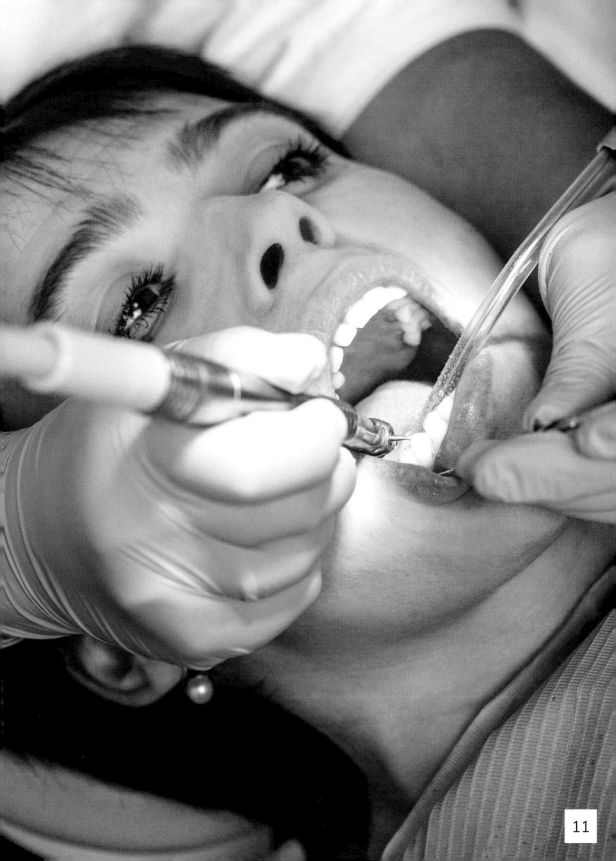

How Dentists Help

Some people don't like to go to the dentist. Dentists try to help them feel more relaxed.

A patient breathing in gas through a mask

Sometimes a dentist uses gas on patients. The dentist puts a small mask over the patient's nose. The gas helps the person to stay calm.

Some dentists go to local schools. They teach kids how to take care of teeth. Dentists talk about food. Snacks and drinks made with lots of sugar can hurt teeth.

They show kids the right way to brush teeth. Some dentists give kids new toothbrushes, toothpaste, or dental floss.

Dentists' Clothes & Tools

Some dentists wear a long, white coat over their clothes. Some wear **scrubs** like a doctor. They wear comfy shoes. Dentists are on their feet a lot.

Dentists try to not spread **germs**. They keep their office and tools clean. They don't want anyone to get sick.

Dentists wear a mask that covers the nose and mouth. They wear glasses to protect their eyes. Dentists wear new gloves for each patient.

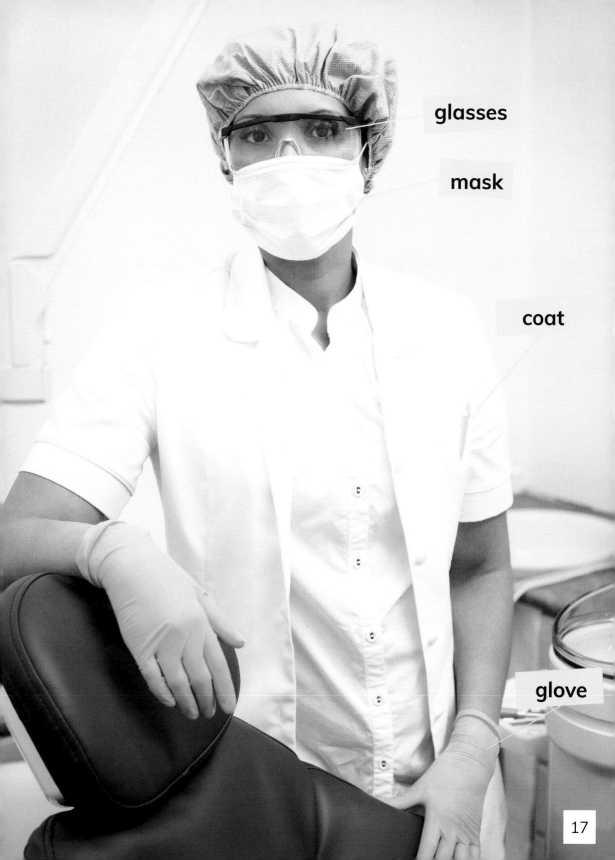

glasses

mask

coat

glove

Dentists use light to look at teeth. A bright light hangs over the patient's chair. Dentists shine light in mouths. They must use long, thin tools. The metal tools reach teeth where hands cannot.

Some of the tools have tiny mirrors. The mirrors help dentists see teeth better.

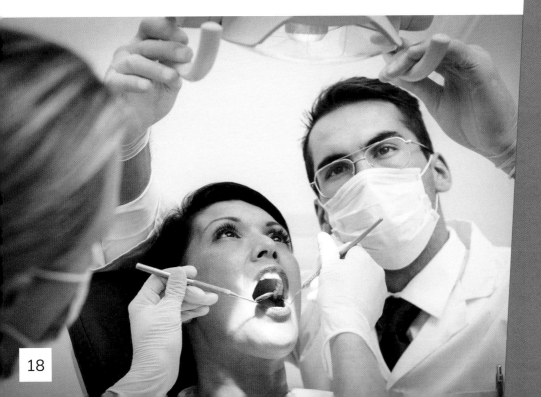

Dentists also take pictures called **X-rays**. The pictures help them see inside teeth, gums, and bones.

Dentists have tools to fix cavities. They use shots to stop someone from feeling pain. They use a drill to remove the cavity.

Where Dentists Work

Most dentists work in small offices called a dental practice. Some work alone. Others work with a group of dentists. Some dentists own their own practice.

Some dentists teach at dental schools. They teach others how to become dentists.

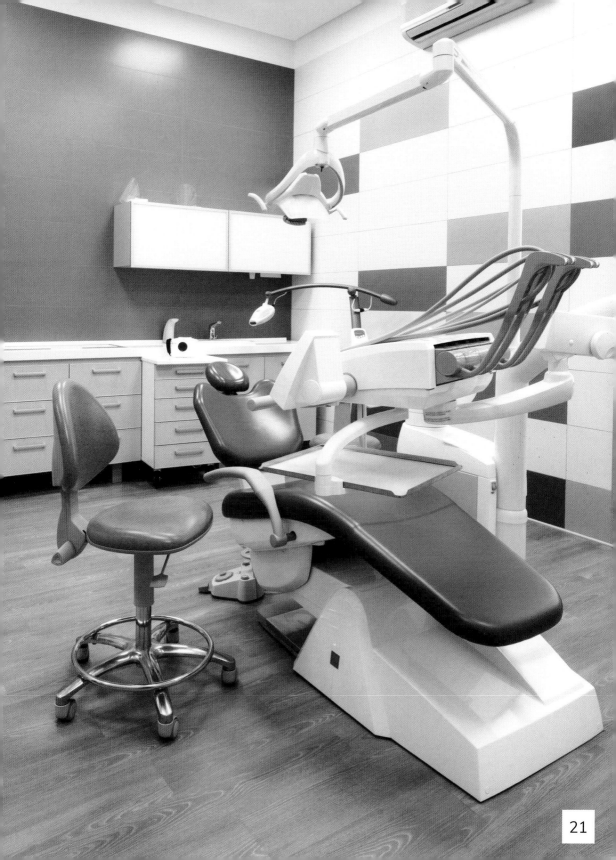

There are nine types of jobs for dentists. Some dentists work only on children's teeth. Some only work on one part of the mouth. They may work only on a patient's gums or jaw bones. They may work only on the roots inside teeth.

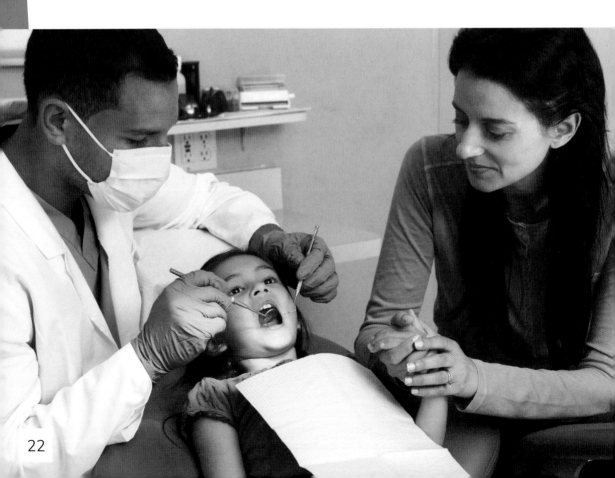

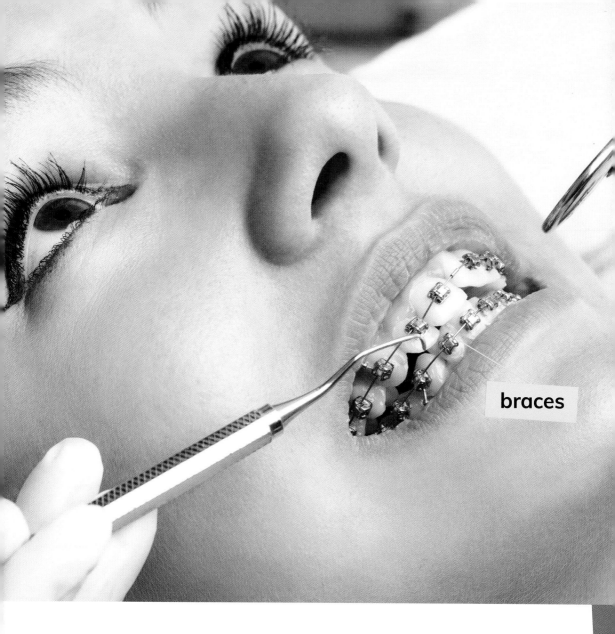

braces

An **orthodontist's** job is to straighten teeth. They place **braces** on teeth. The braces move the teeth.

How to Become a Dentist

Most dentists grew up keeping their teeth clean. Now they want others to have a healthy smile too.

Dentists need a lot of schooling. After high school, they need four years of college. There they study science or pre-dentistry. They take tests to get into dental school.

Dental school takes another four years. There, they learn how to give shots and read X-rays. They also work on patients.

After dental school, they must pass a test. They also have to show they know how to fix problems.

New dentists work for other dentists. They can also own their own dental business.

Famous Dentists

In 1728, a French doctor named Pierre Fauchard wrote a book about dentistry. He was the first person to fill in cavities. He found out that sugar hurts teeth.

The first dentist in the U.S. was John Baker. He came from England to the U.S. in the 1700s. Isaac Greenwood was the first dentist born in the U.S.

Pierre Fauchard

Fast Facts

- **What Dentists Do:**
Dentists care for teeth.

- **Where Dentists Work:**
dental offices or dental schools

- **Key Clothing:**
white coat, scrubs, gloves, glasses, mask

- **Key Tools:**
drills, lights, metal tools, X-rays

- **Education Needed:**
8 years of college

- **Famous Dentists:**
Pierre Fauchard, John Baker, Isaac Greenwood

Glossary

braces (BRAY-sihz)—a device attached to teeth to pull them into position and make them straight

cavity (KA-vuh-tee)—a broken-down part of a tooth

filling (FIL-ing)—material put into a tooth to stop cavities

floss (FLAWS)—a thin strand of thread used to clean in between teeth

germ (JURM)—a tiny living thing that causes sickness

gum (GUHM)—the firm flesh around the base of a person's tooth

healthy (HEL-thee)—teeth that are well taken care of; without cavities or stains

orthodontist (OR-tha-DON-tihst)—a type of dentist who specializes in straightening teeth

scrubs (SCRUHBS)—loose, lightweight uniforms worn by some dentists

sealant (SEEL-uhnt)—a protective substance that goes over teeth to stop cavities from growing

X-ray (EKS-ray)—a picture taken of the inside of the mouth that can show if something is wrong

Read More

Clark, Rosalyn. *Why We Go to the Dentist.* Minneapolis: Lerner Publications, 2018.

Kenan, Tessa. *Hooray for Dentists!* Minneapolis: Lerner Publications, 2018.

Waxman, Laura Hamilton. *Dentist Tools.* Minneapolis: Lerner Publications, 2019.

Internet Sites

How Teeth Work
kidshealth.org/en/kids/teeth-movie.html?WT.ac=k-ra

Dental Games
www.mykoolsmiles.com/content/dental-games-for-kids

National Children's Dental Health Month
www.nidcr.nih.gov/news-events/february-national-childrens-dental-health-month

Index